UNDER THE MICROSCOPE

Brain

Our body's nerve centre

Contributors

Author and series consultant: **Richard Walker BSc PhD PGCE** taught biology, science and health education for several years before becoming a full-time writer. He is a foremost author and consultant specializing in books for adults and children on human biology, health and natural history. He is the author of *Heart: How the blood gets around the body, Making Life: How we reproduce and grow, Muscles: How we move and exercise* and *Brain: Our body's nerve centre* in this series, and is consultant on the whole series.

Advisory panel

1 Heart: How the blood gets around the body
P M Schofield MD FRCP FICA FACC FESC is Consultant Cardiologist at Papworth Hospital, Cambridge

2 Skeleton: Our body's framework
R N Villar MS FRCS is Consultant Orthopaedic Surgeon at Cambridge BUPA Lea Hospital and Addenbrooke's Hospital, Cambridge

3 Digesting: How we fuel the body
J O Hunter FRCP is Director of the Gastroenterology Research Unit, Addenbrooke's Hospital, Cambridge

4 Making Life: How we reproduce and grow
Jane MacDougall MD MRCOG is Consultant Obstetrician and Gynaecologist at the Rosie Maternity Hospital, Addenbrooke's NHS Trust, Cambridge

5 Breathing: How we use air
Mark Slade MA MBBS MRCP is Senior Registrar, Department of Respiratory Medicine, Addenbrooke's Hospital, Cambridge

6 Senses: How we connect with the world
Peter Garrard MA MRCP is Medical Research Council Fellow and Honorary Specialist Registrar, Neurology Department, Addenbrooke's Hospital, Cambridge

7 Muscles: How we move and exercise
Jumbo Jenner MD FRCP is Consultant, and **R T Kavanagh MD MRCP** is Senior Registrar, Department of Rheumatology, Addenbrooke's Hospital, Cambridge

8 Brain: Our body's nerve centre
Peter Garrard MA MRCP is Medical Research Council Fellow and Honorary Specialist Registrar, Neurology Department, Addenbrooke's Hospital, Cambridge

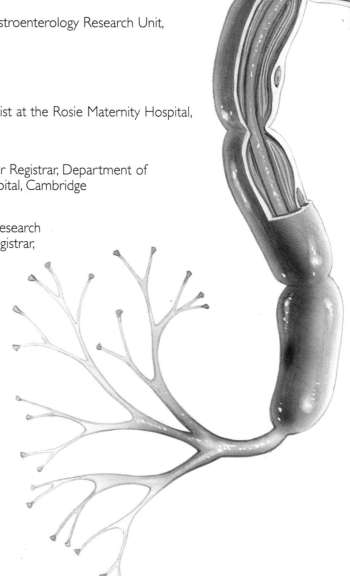

Brain

Our body's nerve centre

Richard Walker

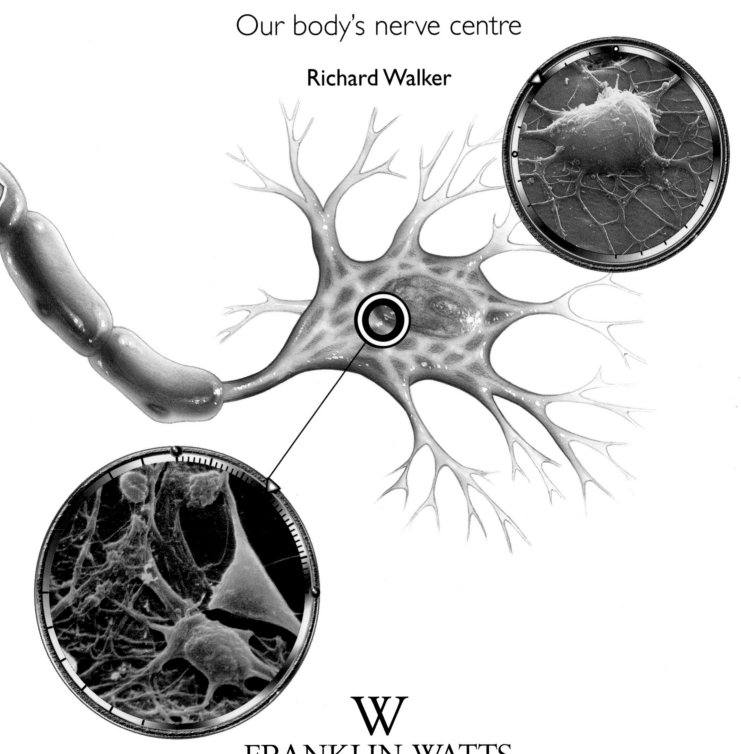

W

FRANKLIN WATTS
NEW YORK • LONDON • SYDNEY

ABOUT THIS BOOK

First published in 1998

Franklin Watts
96 Leonard Street
London EC2A 4RH

Franklin Watts Australia
14 Mars Road
Lane Cove
NSW 2066

© Franklin Watts 1998

0 7496 3083 3

Dewey Decimal Classification Number: 612.8

A CIP catalogue record for this book is
available from the British Library

Printed in Belgium

Produced for Franklin Watts
by Miles Kelly Publishing
Unit 11
The Bardfield Centre
Great Bardfield
Essex
CM7 4SL

Designed by Full Steam Ahead

Illustrated by Roger Stewart

Picture research by Elaine Willis

Under the Microscope uses micro-photography to allow you to see right inside the human body.

The camera acts as a microscope, looking at unseen parts of the body and zooming in on the body's cells at work. Some micro-photographs are magnified hundreds of times, others thousands of times. They have been dramatically coloured to bring details into crisp focus, and are linked to clear and accurate illustrations that fit them in context inside the body.

New words are explained the first time that they are used, and can also be checked in the glossary at the back of the book.

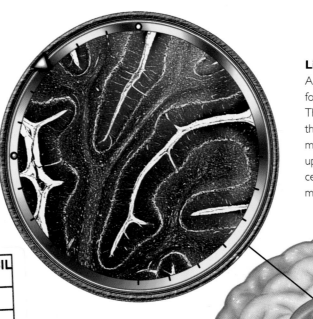

Little brain
A view inside the cerebellum (left), found at the rear of the brain (below). The cerebellum is sometimes called the 'little brain' to contrast it with the massive, folded cerebrum that makes up most of the rest of the brain. The cerebellum helps you balance and move in a co-ordinated fashion.

4

CONTENTS

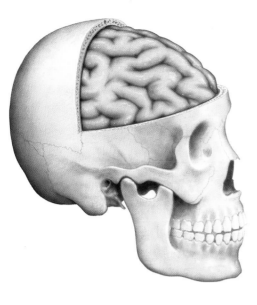

INTRODUCTION

Every country in the world has a government. The government makes laws that control the country, so that people can live together in peace. Without a government there would be chaos.

Think of the human body like a country. It consists of billions of cells. Cells of the same type form tissues. Different tissues make up organs such as the stomach or eye. Organs are linked together into systems, such as the digestive system. All these systems make up the body. For the body to function, its cells, tissues, organs and systems have to work together. Like a country, the body needs a government to make it run smoothly.

The brain is at the core of the body's government. The brain keeps the body in order. It regulates many body processes by controlling the functioning of organs and systems. It also enables us to feel, think, imagine, create, remember, have a personality and be sad or happy — to behave like human beings and as individuals.

The brain communicates with the rest of the body through the spinal cord and a wiring system formed by the nerves. The spinal cord and nerves relay information to the brain to keep it updated about everything happening inside and outside the body. And they relay instructions to all parts of the body telling them what to do and when to do it.

One other body system works with the brain and nerves to keep the body in a balanced state. This is the endocrine or hormonal system. It releases chemicals called hormones into the bloodstream, and they carry instructions to all parts of the body.

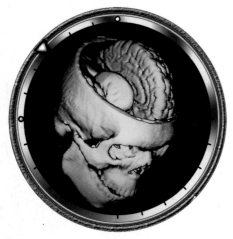

Brain in place
This special type of X-ray, called a CT scan, shows a person's brain in place in their skull. The computer that produces the scan has 'removed' the top of the skull to reveal the left half of the brain.

Thinking cells
Your brain contains hundreds of billions of nerve cells. This micrograph shows just a few. Brain cells connect with each other to make a very complex system which lets you feel, think and make decisions.

Brain slice
This Magnetic Resonance Imaging (MRI) scan (right) shows a section, in side view, of a person's brain. You can see the outline of the head, and the brain protected by the skull. The spinal cord links the brain to the rest of the body.

Neuron close-up
Many nerve cells are very long because they have to carry messages over long distances. This micrograph (right) shows one end of a motor neuron, a type of nerve cell that carries instructions from the brain and spinal cord to the muscles and glands.

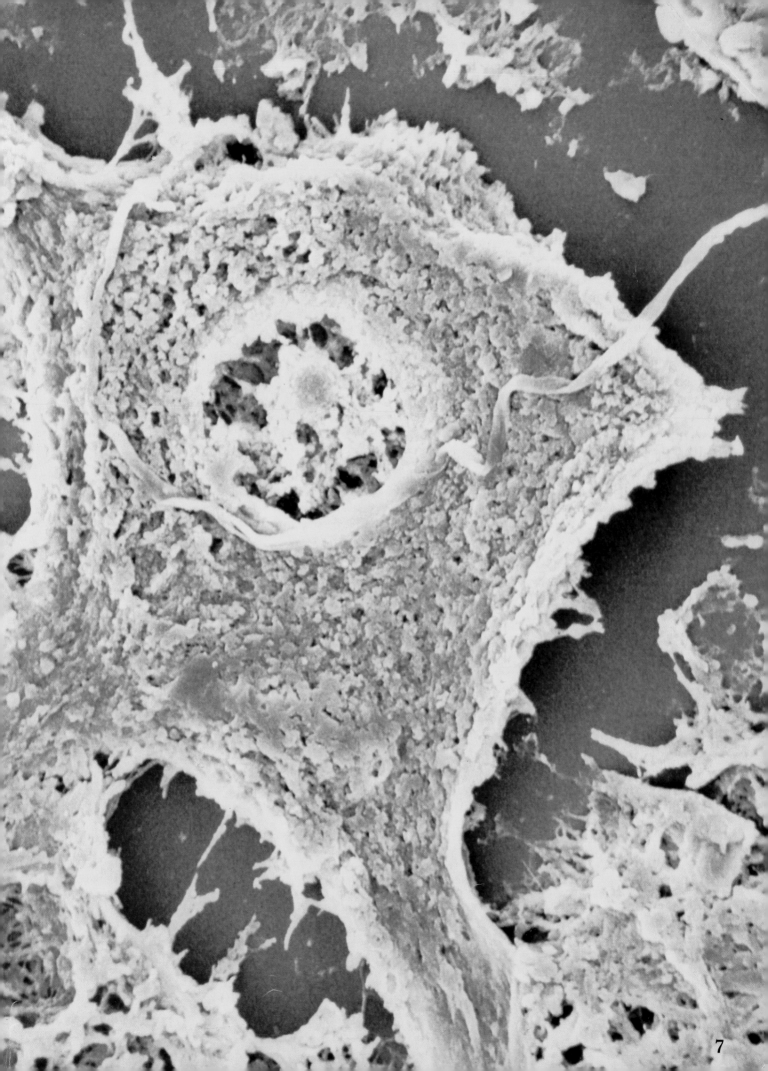

7

THE NERVOUS SYSTEM

The nervous system plays a major role in co-ordinating and controlling the body's activities. It is made up of billions of nerve cells. These cells are linked to form a massive communications network. Nerve cells carry messages in the form of electrical impulses. These impulses are carried at high speed around the body to keep it safe and functioning normally.

The nervous system is usually divided into two main parts: the central nervous system (CNS) and the peripheral (outer) nervous system. The spinal cord and the brain make up the CNS. The job of the CNS is to receive information from all parts of the body, to analyse and store that information, and to send out instructions based upon it. The peripheral nervous system consists of the nerves that ferry information from all parts of the body to the CNS, and back from the CNS to various parts of the body.

Here is a simple example of how the nervous system works. A car is speeding towards you. Your eyes send messages along nerves to your brain. In a split-second, your brain recalls previous experiences of fast-moving objects. It sends high-speed instructions down your spinal cord and along another nerve to your leg muscles. These muscles move you quickly out of the way of the car, which speeds past.

Central nervous system: brain and spinal cord

Sensory neurons

Motor neurons

Motor neurons of somatic nervous system (control muscles)

Motor neurons of autonomic nervous system (control automatic functions)

Sympathetic nervous system

Parasympathetic nervous system

Parts of the nervous system

The nervous system is divided into the central nervous system (brain and spinal cord) and the peripheral nervous system (the nerves). The peripheral nervous system has three parts. Sensory neurons (nerve cells) relay information to the CNS about what is happening inside and outside the body. Motor neurons of the **somatic** nervous system carry instructions from the CNS to muscles telling them to move specific parts of the body. Motor neurons of the **autonomic** nervous system carry instructions from the CNS to the body's organs and glands; these instructions control automatic functions such as breathing and heart rate. The autonomic nervous system has two parts, called the sympathetic and parasympathetic systems.

The nervous system

The nervous system consists of the brain, the spinal cord and the nerves. The nerves spread out from the brain and spinal cord to reach all parts of the body. There are twelve pairs of cranial nerves that come from the brain, and 31 pairs of spinal nerves that come from the spinal cord.

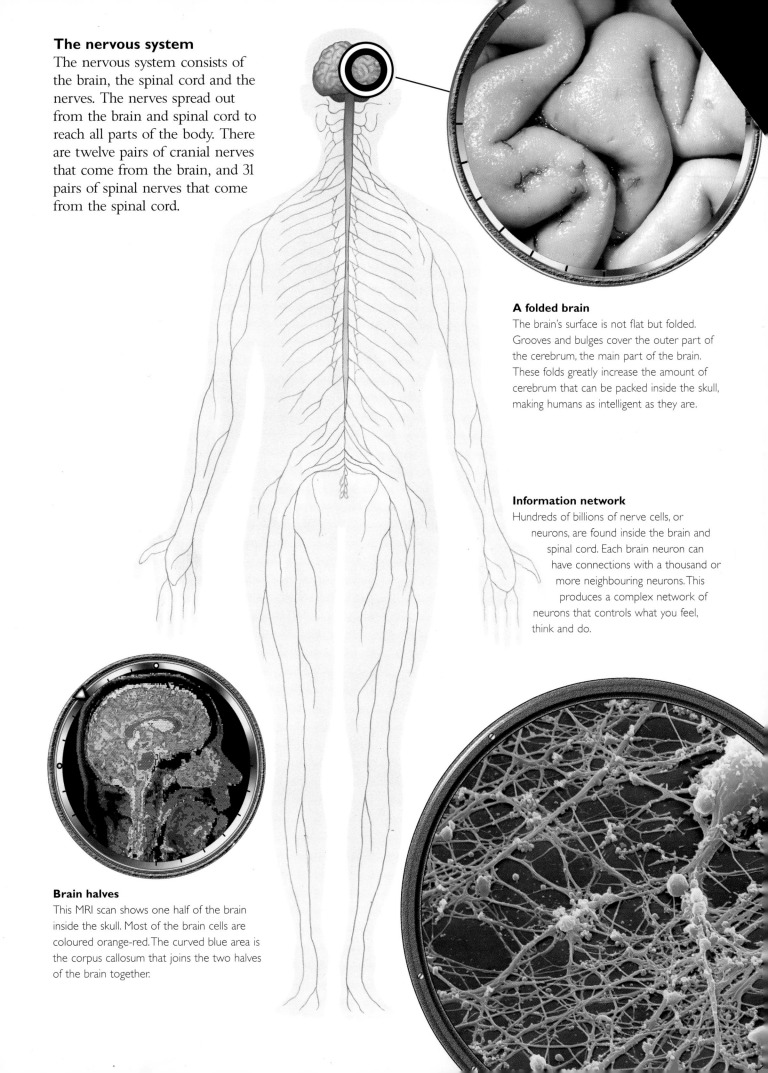

A folded brain

The brain's surface is not flat but folded. Grooves and bulges cover the outer part of the cerebrum, the main part of the brain. These folds greatly increase the amount of cerebrum that can be packed inside the skull, making humans as intelligent as they are.

Information network

Hundreds of billions of nerve cells, or neurons, are found inside the brain and spinal cord. Each brain neuron can have connections with a thousand or more neighbouring neurons. This produces a complex network of neurons that controls what you feel, think and do.

Brain halves

This MRI scan shows one half of the brain inside the skull. Most of the brain cells are coloured orange-red. The curved blue area is the corpus callosum that joins the two halves of the brain together.

Nerves are the 'wires' of the nervous system. They run from the central nervous system (CNS) – the brain and spinal cord – to all parts of the body including bones, muscles and skin. Nerves divide many times as they fan out from the CNS so that they can make contact with all parts of the body. The thickest nerves – such as the sciatic nerve which is 2 centimetres (1 inch) wide where it begins the spinal cord – are creamy in colour and look like shiny ropes; the thinnest nerves are thinner than a human hair.

Dendrites
(carry impulses from
neighbouring cells)

Cell body

Each nerve is coated in a tough fibrous sheath and contains bundles of hundreds or thousands of nerve cells called neurons. Neurons are long, very thin cells. They run along the nerve like the thin copper wires in a power cable. Neurons carry electrical messages called nerve impulses.

There are three types of neurons. Sensory and motor neurons relay nerve impulses to and from the CNS; association neurons relay information from sensory to motor neurons within the CNS. Most nerves contain a mixture of both sensory and motor neurons. Sensory neurons make up the sensory part of the peripheral nervous system; motor neurons make up both the motor and autonomic parts of the peripheral nervous system.

Unlike most body cells, neurons cannot divide to replace themselves as they wear out. Nervous tissue has very limited powers of repair if it is damaged by disease or injury. This is especially true of the brain and spinal cord.

Axon

Axon terminal
where motor
neuron meets
muscle

Motor neuron
Like many neurons, this motor neuron has a cell body that receives nerve impulses (messages) along fine branches, called dendrites, from other neurons. The cell body is found inside the brain or spinal cord. A long axon carries nerve impulses from the cell body to the muscles and other parts of the body.

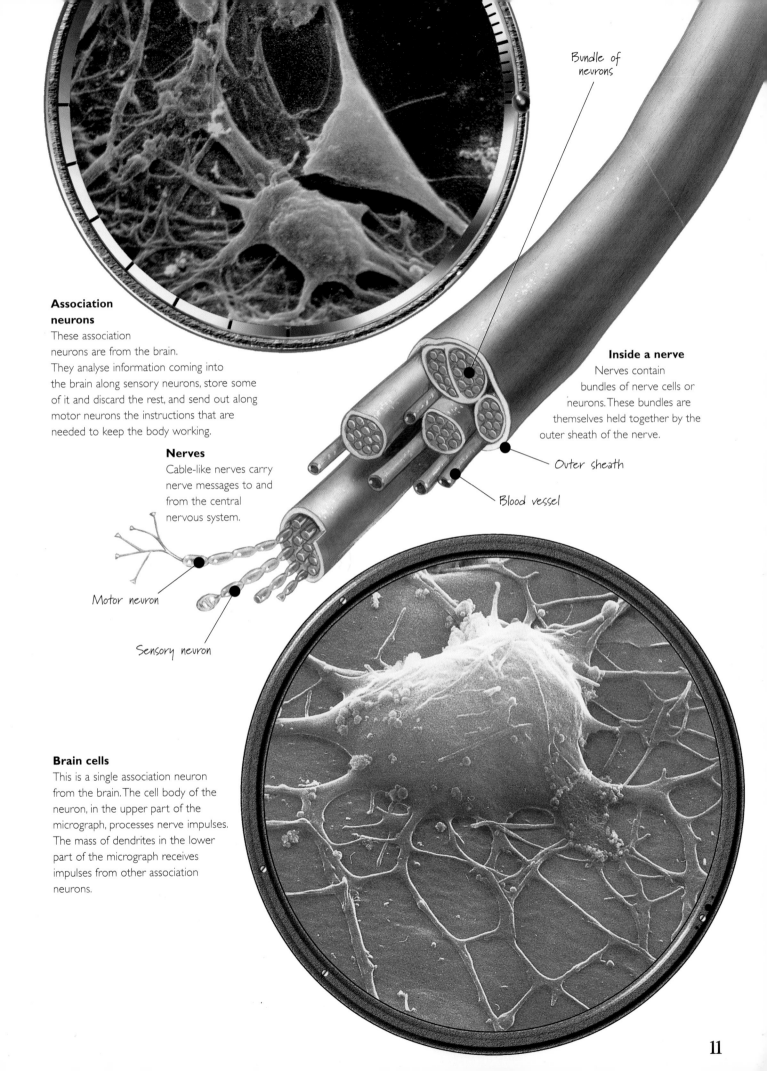

Association neurons

These association neurons are from the brain. They analyse information coming into the brain along sensory neurons, store some of it and discard the rest, and send out along motor neurons the instructions that are needed to keep the body working.

Bundle of neurons

Inside a nerve

Nerves contain bundles of nerve cells or neurons. These bundles are themselves held together by the outer sheath of the nerve.

Outer sheath

Blood vessel

Nerves

Cable-like nerves carry nerve messages to and from the central nervous system.

Motor neuron

Sensory neuron

Brain cells

This is a single association neuron from the brain. The cell body of the neuron, in the upper part of the micrograph, processes nerve impulses. The mass of dendrites in the lower part of the micrograph receives impulses from other association neurons.

NERVE SIGNALS

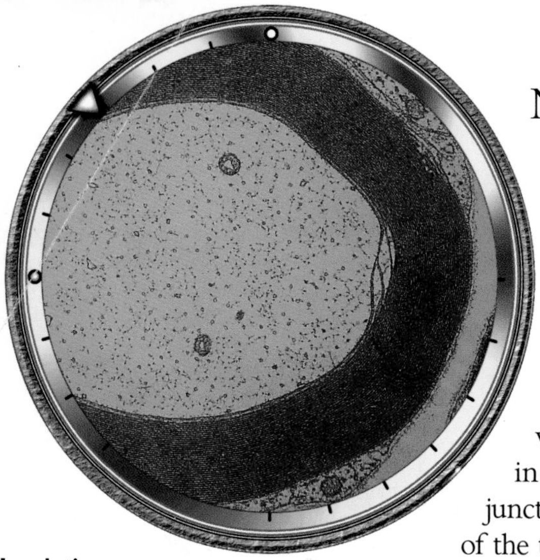

Neurons are nerve cells. They carry nerve messages or impulses in the form of a tiny electrical charge.

The electrical charge travels along the neuron at speeds of up to 100 metres (330 feet) per second. Neurons transmit an impulse when they receive a stimulus. It could be light entering the eye, a change in body temperature or an impulse arriving from a neighbouring neuron. If the stimulus is strong enough it will trigger a nerve impulse. This races along the neuron, always in the same direction. Two neurons meet – but do not touch – at a junction called a synapse. There is a tiny gap between the fine endings of the two neurons. The impulse does not 'jump' the gap as an electrical signal. Instead, the synapse releases chemicals which cross the gap. For a moment the impulse becomes a chemical signal. When this reaches the next neuron it triggers a nerve impulse which carries the message onwards.

Insulation

Some neurons are insulated by a myelin sheath. This is a fatty covering formed by neuroglial (support) cells called Schwann cells. These wrap themselves tightly around certain nerve fibres and insulate them. This makes nerve impulses travel even faster.

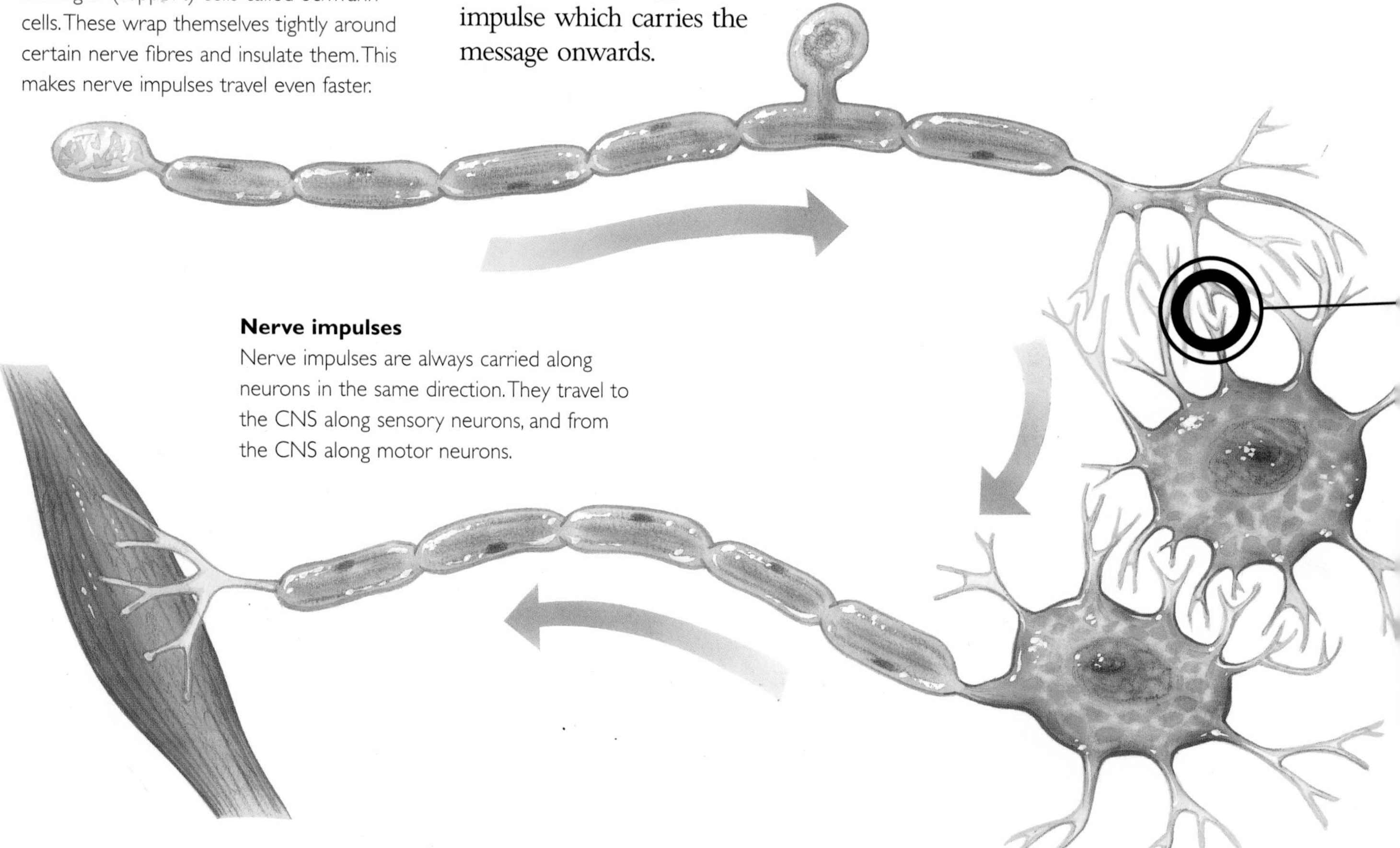

Nerve impulses

Nerve impulses are always carried along neurons in the same direction. They travel to the CNS along sensory neurons, and from the CNS along motor neurons.

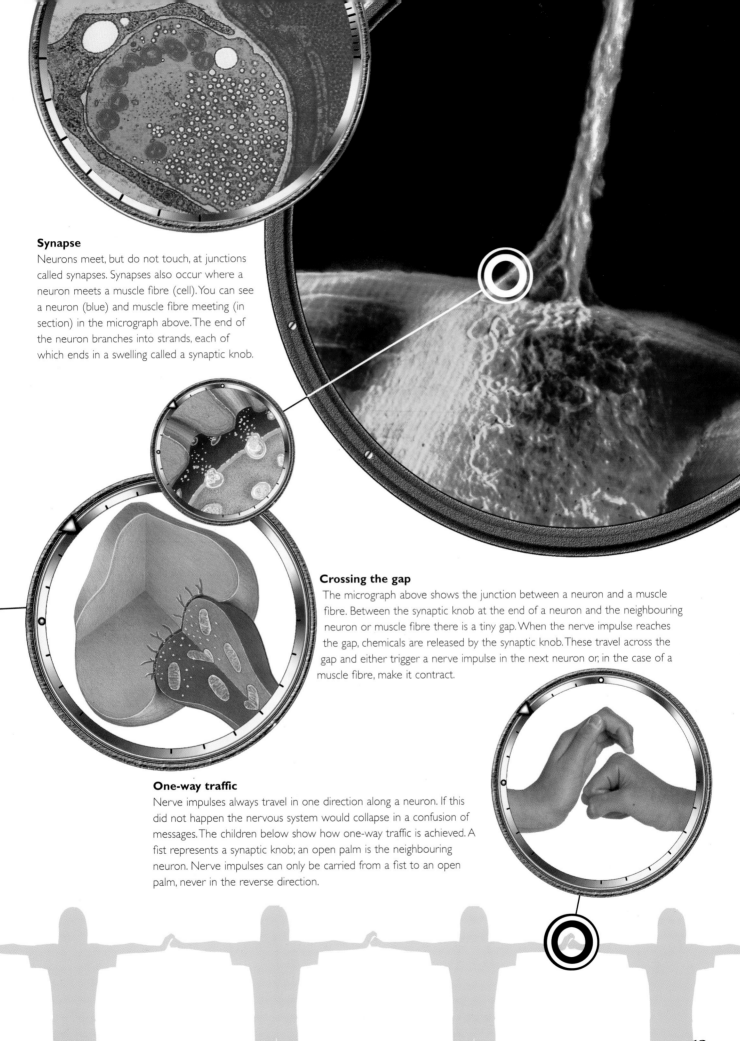

Synapse

Neurons meet, but do not touch, at junctions called synapses. Synapses also occur where a neuron meets a muscle fibre (cell). You can see a neuron (blue) and muscle fibre meeting (in section) in the micrograph above. The end of the neuron branches into strands, each of which ends in a swelling called a synaptic knob.

Crossing the gap

The micrograph above shows the junction between a neuron and a muscle fibre. Between the synaptic knob at the end of a neuron and the neighbouring neuron or muscle fibre there is a tiny gap. When the nerve impulse reaches the gap, chemicals are released by the synaptic knob. These travel across the gap and either trigger a nerve impulse in the next neuron or, in the case of a muscle fibre, make it contract.

One-way traffic

Nerve impulses always travel in one direction along a neuron. If this did not happen the nervous system would collapse in a confusion of messages. The children below show how one-way traffic is achieved. A fist represents a synaptic knob; an open palm is the neighbouring neuron. Nerve impulses can only be carried from a fist to an open palm, never in the reverse direction.

THE SPINAL CORD

The spinal cord is the main communications highway of the nervous system. It is a flattened cylinder of nerve cells. In an adult, the spinal cord is about 43 centimetres (17 inches) long, and as thick as a finger at its widest point. It runs down the back of the body from the base of the brain, tapering to a thread-like tail in the lower back. Like other parts of the nervous system, the spinal cord cannot repair itself if it is cut or damaged.

The job of the spinal cord is to relay information between the body and the brain. The spinal cord receives information from the body — carried by sensory neurons inside spinal nerves — and relays it to the brain. It relays information from the brain to motor neurons — inside spinal nerves — which carry instructions to the body. The spinal cord also plays a key role in many reflex actions. These are actions that we perform without thinking, and which enable us to react rapidly to danger.

Spinal section
This micrograph shows a section cut across the spinal cord. You can see the H-shaped central part called the grey matter, which contains the cell bodies of neurons, and the outer white matter, which contains the axons of neurons.

Bony protection
The backbone, or spine, consists of a chain of bones called vertebrae. The hole through each vertebra makes up the vertebral canal. When vertebrae are joined together in the backbone, their combined vertebral canals form a bony tunnel. The spinal cord runs along this tunnel protected by a covering of bone. Spinal nerves emerge through gaps between adjacent vertebrae.

Inside the spinal cord

The spinal cord has two main parts. The inner, H-shaped grey matter contains association neurons that relay information between the spinal cord and spinal nerves. The outer white matter consists of nerve fibres (axons) that form nerve tracts which relay information up or down the spinal cord, to or from the brain. Three membranes (the meninges) around the spinal cord protect it. A liquid called cerebrospinal fluid flows between the inner and middle membranes. It nourishes the spinal cord and acts as a shock absorber. Sensory nerve fibres enter the back of the spinal cord from a spinal nerve; motor nerve fibres leave the front of the spinal cord to join a spinal nerve.

Grey matter

Spinal nerve

Spinal cord and spinal nerves

The spinal cord runs from the brain to just over halfway down the back. The delicate tissue of the spinal cord is protected within the backbone. Nerves emerge from the spinal cord at regular intervals, usually with the motor part of the nerve towards the front and the sensory part towards the back. In the neck and lower back the spinal nerves join to form junctions, each called a plexus, where the major nerves originate.

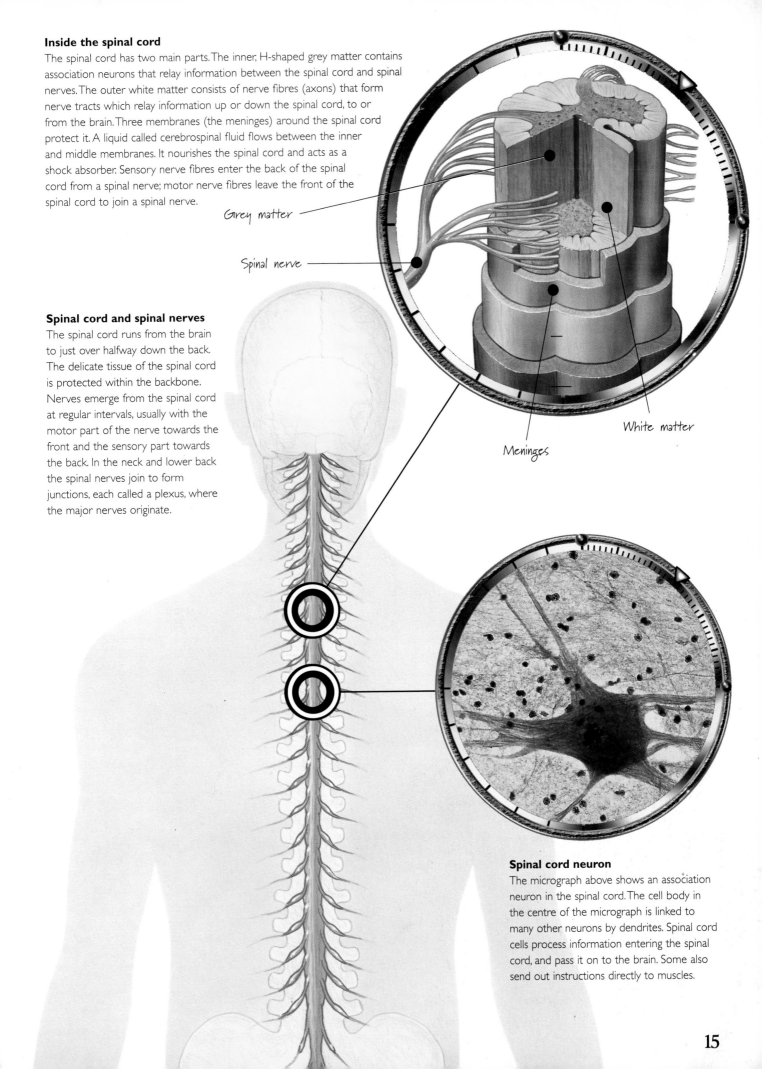

Meninges

White matter

Spinal cord neuron

The micrograph above shows an association neuron in the spinal cord. The cell body in the centre of the micrograph is linked to many other neurons by dendrites. Spinal cord cells process information entering the spinal cord, and pass it on to the brain. Some also send out instructions directly to muscles.

REFLEXES

A reflex is a split-second, automatic response to a stimulus. Reflexes are rapid and unchanging. The response shown during a reflex action is totally predictable. Many reflex actions protect the body from harm or danger. These include blinking, making the pupils smaller to prevent light from damaging the eye, and withdrawing a hand from something hot or sharp. Other reflexes include swallowing, which happens automatically when food touches the back of the throat.

Reflexes happen very quickly because the impulses that produce them travel along the shortest possible nerve pathway. This pathway is called a reflex arc. In most cases, the reflex arc passes through the spinal cord only, bypassing the brain. Sending nerve impulses to the brain would use up valuable time. This is why reflex actions happen without us thinking about them. By the time we are aware of them the danger has hopefully been avoided.

Nerve-muscle junction

A motor neuron (the thin branched structure) meets skeletal muscle fibres (the striped cylinders). Skeletal muscles move the body when they receive instructions carried by motor neurons. During a reflex action, instructions telling the muscle to contract commonly arrive from the spinal cord.

Reflex action

If you touch something hot or sharp you automatically pull your hand away without thinking about it. This is a type of reflex action called a withdrawal reflex.

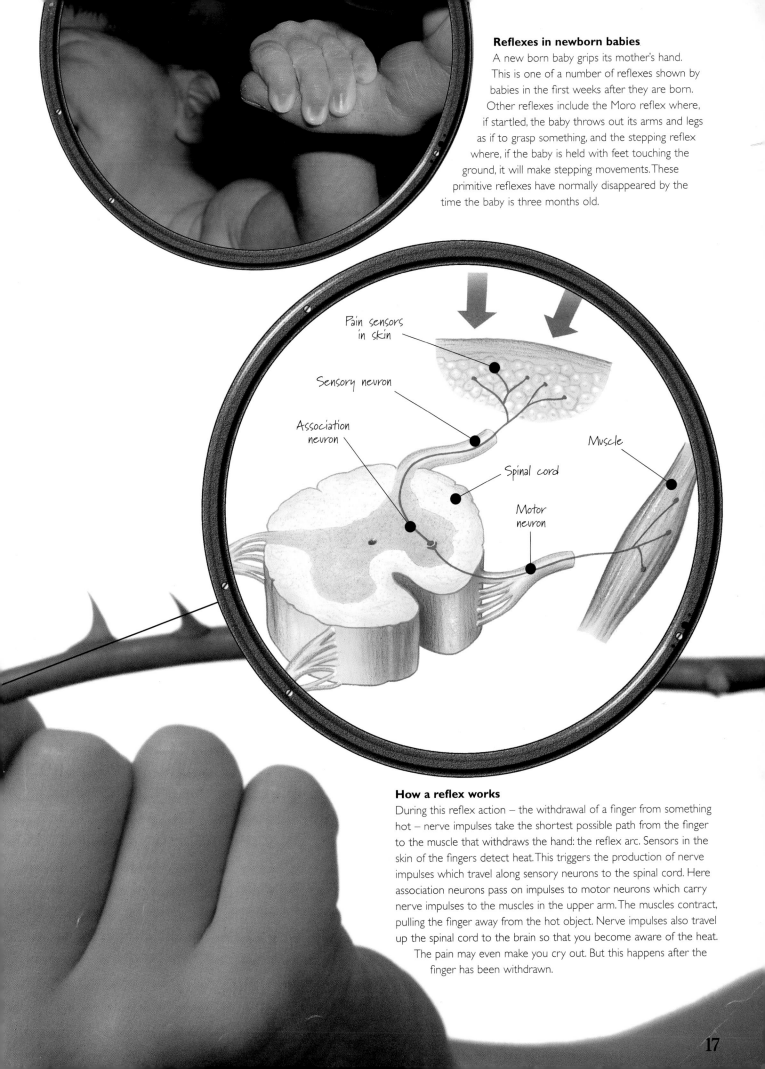

Reflexes in newborn babies

A new born baby grips its mother's hand. This is one of a number of reflexes shown by babies in the first weeks after they are born. Other reflexes include the Moro reflex where, if startled, the baby throws out its arms and legs as if to grasp something, and the stepping reflex where, if the baby is held with feet touching the ground, it will make stepping movements. These primitive reflexes have normally disappeared by the time the baby is three months old.

Pain sensors in skin

Sensory neuron

Association neuron

Spinal cord

Muscle

Motor neuron

How a reflex works

During this reflex action – the withdrawal of a finger from something hot – nerve impulses take the shortest possible path from the finger to the muscle that withdraws the hand: the reflex arc. Sensors in the skin of the fingers detect heat. This triggers the production of nerve impulses which travel along sensory neurons to the spinal cord. Here association neurons pass on impulses to motor neurons which carry nerve impulses to the muscles in the upper arm. The muscles contract, pulling the finger away from the hot object. Nerve impulses also travel up the spinal cord to the brain so that you become aware of the heat. The pain may even make you cry out. But this happens after the finger has been withdrawn.

THE BRAIN & THE BODY

The brain is the control centre of the nervous system. It gives us our personality, and enables us to think and feel. It also sends out instructions that control the way we move, as well as regulating how quickly we breathe and how fast our heart beats, for example.

The brain consists of hundreds of billions of nerve cells. Many are association neurons, whose job is constantly to receive and transmit nerve impulses. Any one of these can have links to hundreds or thousands of other neurons. This produces a network of unimaginable complexity, with trillions of connections. The workings of this network, which enable us to behave and communicate in very many ways, make the most advanced computer appear simple. A man's brain weighs on average 1.6 kilograms (3.5 pounds); a woman's about 1.45 kilograms (3.2 pounds). The difference is because men tend to be larger and heavier than women. There is no link between brain size and intelligence. Intelligence depends on the number and complexity of the connections between the billions of brain cells.

Brain control

The brain controls almost all aspects of the body's activities. These include conscious actions such as riding a bicycle, jumping a hurdle or writing a letter; and all those things that happen automatically, such as feeling hungry or thirsty, or breathing faster during a race.

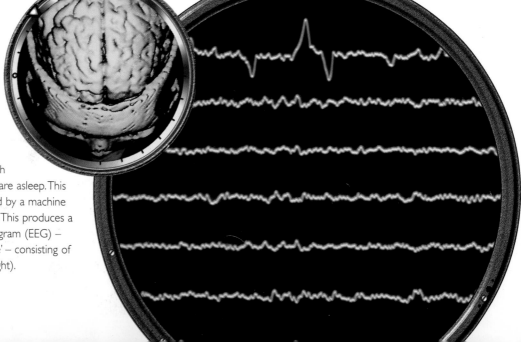

Brain waves

The billions of cells in the brain (above right) constantly buzz with electrical activity even when we are asleep. This electrical activity can be detected by a machine called an electroencephalograph. This produces a trace called an electroencephalogram (EEG) – literally an 'electrical head picture' – consisting of wavy lines called brain waves (right).

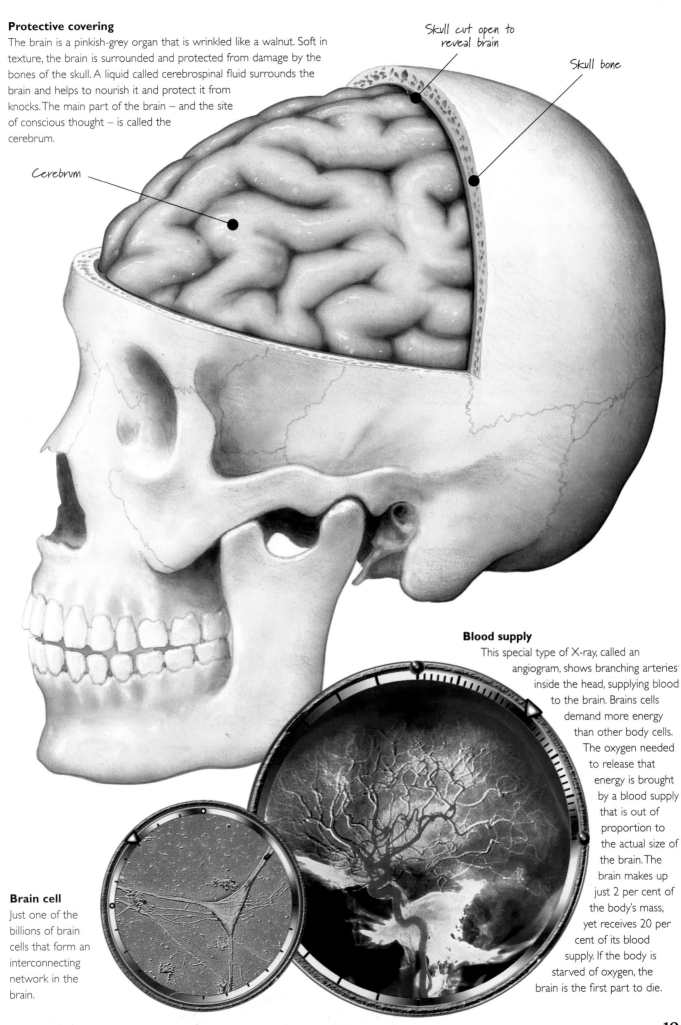

Protective covering

The brain is a pinkish-grey organ that is wrinkled like a walnut. Soft in texture, the brain is surrounded and protected from damage by the bones of the skull. A liquid called cerebrospinal fluid surrounds the brain and helps to nourish it and protect it from knocks. The main part of the brain – and the site of conscious thought – is called the cerebrum.

Cerebrum

Skull cut open to reveal brain

Skull bone

Blood supply

This special type of X-ray, called an angiogram, shows branching arteries inside the head, supplying blood to the brain. Brains cells demand more energy than other body cells. The oxygen needed to release that energy is brought by a blood supply that is out of proportion to the actual size of the brain. The brain makes up just 2 per cent of the body's mass, yet receives 20 per cent of its blood supply. If the body is starved of oxygen, the brain is the first part to die.

Brain cell

Just one of the billions of brain cells that form an interconnecting network in the brain.

PARTS OF THE BRAIN

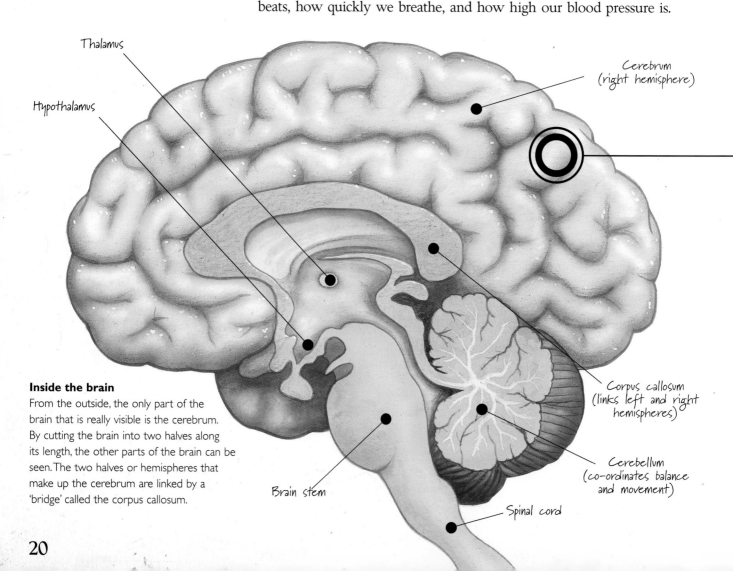

Two halves

A human brain held in gloved hands. You can see from this front view of the brain that the main part of the brain, the wrinkled cerebrum, is divided into two halves or hemispheres.

The brain is divided into three main regions, each with different functions. These regions are the forebrain, the cerebellum and the brain stem.

The forebrain has four parts: the cerebrum, the thalamus, the hypothalamus and the limbic system (see page 32). The cerebrum is the largest part of the brain and makes up about 85 per cent of its mass. It is responsible for conscious thoughts and actions. The thalamus is an information relay station. It sorts, analyses and discards nerve messages, and relays them between the spinal cord and the cerebrum. The hypothalamus controls many automatic body processes such as body temperature and hunger. The limbic system controls our feelings and emotions.

The cerebellum controls the body's balance and co-ordination, while the brain stem forms a link between brain and spinal cord. It monitors and regulates the body's vital functions. These include how fast the heart beats, how quickly we breathe, and how high our blood pressure is.

Thalamus

Hypothalamus

Cerebrum (right hemisphere)

Corpus callosum (links left and right hemispheres)

Cerebellum (co-ordinates balance and movement)

Brain stem

Spinal cord

Inside the brain

From the outside, the only part of the brain that is really visible is the cerebrum. By cutting the brain into two halves along its length, the other parts of the brain can be seen. The two halves or hemispheres that make up the cerebrum are linked by a 'bridge' called the corpus callosum.

Inside the cerebellum

This micrograph (right) shows the layers of nerve cells inside the cerebellum, found at the back of the brain. The cerebellum works with the cerebrum and other parts of the brain to make sure that you keep your balance and that the movements you make are smooth and not jerky.

Ventricles

Brain ventricles

Inside the brain are a series of spaces called ventricles. The ventricles produce a liquid called cerebrospinal fluid. This moves around the brain, protecting it from knocks and supplying brain cells with food.

Across the brain

This MRI scan (above) shows a slice through the human brain as seen from the top of the head. It shows the cerebrum divided into two hemispheres, right and left. The spaces in the middle of the brain are the ventricles that produce cerebrospinal fluid.

Brain and brain stem

A side view of the head and neck using an MRI scanner reveals the brain and brain stem. The brain stem (blue) connects the spinal cord to the higher parts of the brain in the cerebrum, which can be seen folded at the top.

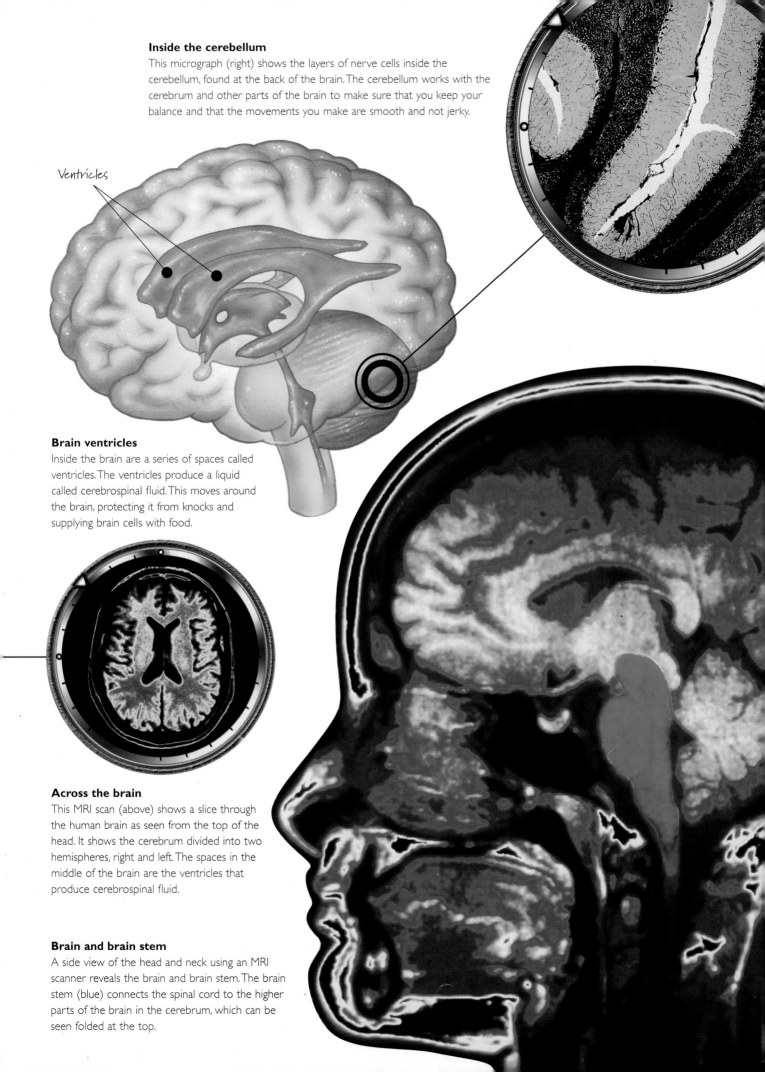

THE CEREBRUM

The cerebrum is divided into left and right halves or hemispheres. The surface of each hemisphere is heavily folded, like the surface of a walnut.

To understand why it is folded like this, we have to look inside the cerebrum. Like the spinal cord, the brain consists of grey matter and white matter. Unlike the spinal cord, the brain's grey matter is on the outside, and white matter on the inside. The outer layer of grey matter, called the cerebral cortex, is just 4 millimetres (0.17 inches) thick. Although the cerebral cortex is thin, its folds and grooves provide for a large surface area of grey matter within the small space inside the skull. In fact, the folded layer of cerebral cortex forms about 40 per cent of the brain's mass.

Different parts of the cerebral cortex perform different tasks, although these may overlap. The cortex can be 'mapped' to show which area is concerned with what body activity.

Healthy brain

This CT scan shows the middle part of a healthy brain in side view. The front of the brain is on the left. You can see clearly the folds covering the right half of the cerebrum, and also how much of the brain the cerebrum occupies. CT scans such as this are used by doctors to look for any possible disorders in the brain. Without the scans, doctors would have to use surgery to look inside the brain.

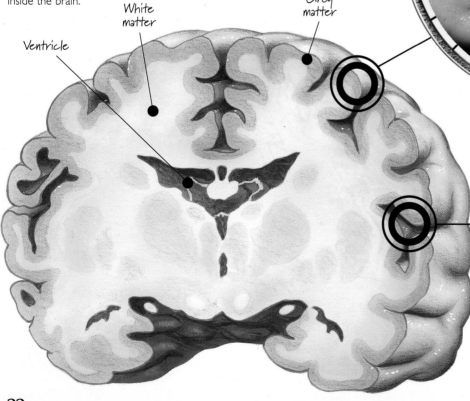

Ventricle

White matter

Grey matter

The cerebrum

The cerebrum is what gives humans their intelligence and complex behaviour. The cerebral cortex, its folded outer surface, enables a lot of 'thinking tissue' to be crammed into the skull.

Grey and white matter

This section cut downwards through the cerebrum shows an outer layer of grey matter (the cerebral cortex) and an inner mass of white matter. In the cerebral cortex we feel pain, store memories, see colours, solve problems, understand language, and tell muscles to contract. The white matter consists of nerve fibres that link the cerebral cortex to other parts of the brain.

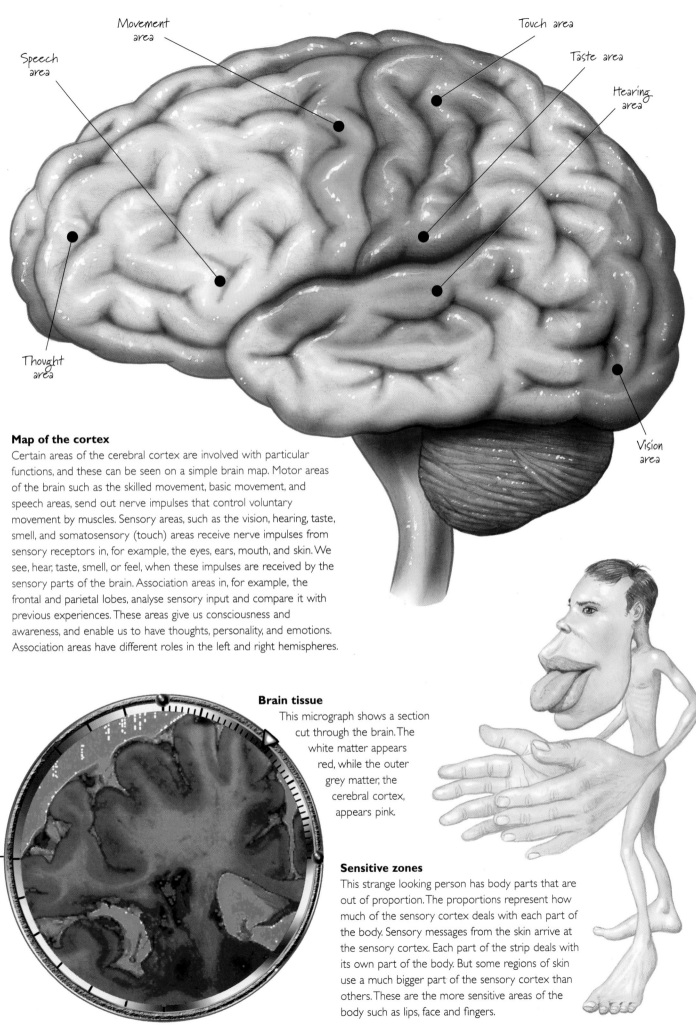

Speech area

Movement area

Touch area

Taste area

Hearing area

Thought area

Vision area

Map of the cortex

Certain areas of the cerebral cortex are involved with particular functions, and these can be seen on a simple brain map. Motor areas of the brain such as the skilled movement, basic movement, and speech areas, send out nerve impulses that control voluntary movement by muscles. Sensory areas, such as the vision, hearing, taste, smell, and somatosensory (touch) areas receive nerve impulses from sensory receptors in, for example, the eyes, ears, mouth, and skin. We see, hear, taste, smell, or feel, when these impulses are received by the sensory parts of the brain. Association areas in, for example, the frontal and parietal lobes, analyse sensory input and compare it with previous experiences. These areas give us consciousness and awareness, and enable us to have thoughts, personality, and emotions. Association areas have different roles in the left and right hemispheres.

Brain tissue

This micrograph shows a section cut through the brain. The white matter appears red, while the outer grey matter, the cerebral cortex, appears pink.

Sensitive zones

This strange looking person has body parts that are out of proportion. The proportions represent how much of the sensory cortex deals with each part of the body. Sensory messages from the skin arrive at the sensory cortex. Each part of the strip deals with its own part of the body. But some regions of skin use a much bigger part of the sensory cortex than others. These are the more sensitive areas of the body such as lips, face and fingers.

LEFT & RIGHT HEMISPHERES

The cerebrum is divided lengthways into two halves, called cerebral hemispheres. Each hemisphere controls the opposite side of the body.

The left hemisphere receives and processes nerve impulses from sensors in the right hand side of the body. It then sends out instructions to muscles and other organs in the right hand side of the body. The right cerebral hemisphere controls the left side of the body in the same way. If you move your left arm, for example, the instructions for that movement come from the right side of your brain. This is because nerve fibres cross from one side to the other at the top of the spinal cord. Those from the left side of the body go to the right side of the brain, and vice versa.

There are differences between the two cerebral hemispheres. The left hemisphere is responsible for mathematical and word skills, while the right hemisphere is responsible for musical and artistic skills. In 90 per cent of people, the left cerebral hemisphere is responsible for written and spoken language, and for the fine control of the hand. This is why most people are right-handed. In the remaining 10 per cent, fine hand movement is controlled by the right cerebral hemisphere, and they are left-handed.

Cerebral hemispheres

Seen from above, the cerebrum is divided into two halves or hemispheres by a deep groove called the longitudinal fissure. In fact, the two hemispheres are not separate. They are connected by a 'bridge' of over 100 million nerve fibres called the corpus callosum.

Left and right activities

As well as controlling opposite sides of the body, left and right sides of the brain have different skills. The left side of the brain deals with numbers, words, problem-solving and reasoning, and scientific skills.

The right side of the brain deals with creativity, recognition of faces and other three-dimensional shapes, artistic and musical activities, insight and imagination, and understanding things as a whole.

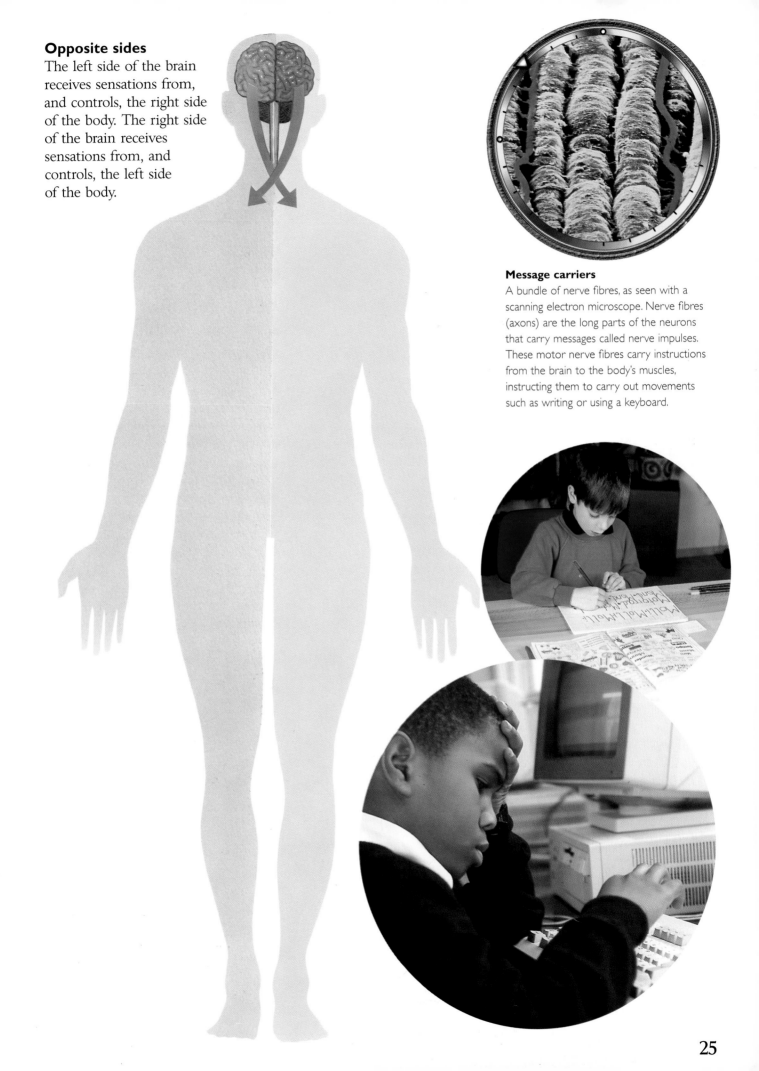

Opposite sides

The left side of the brain receives sensations from, and controls, the right side of the body. The right side of the brain receives sensations from, and controls, the left side of the body.

Message carriers

A bundle of nerve fibres, as seen with a scanning electron microscope. Nerve fibres (axons) are the long parts of the neurons that carry messages called nerve impulses. These motor nerve fibres carry instructions from the brain to the body's muscles, instructing them to carry out movements such as writing or using a keyboard.

THE BRAIN, PERSONALITY & THINKING

Different parts of the cerebrum have different roles. One part enables us to see the world around us; another lets us smell delicious food; another controls our movements.

But which part of the brain makes us who we are: intelligent, thinking individuals, each with our own personality? Scientists and doctors have spent many years trying to find out. They believe that all parts of the brain contribute to our individuality. But the areas that create connections or associations − by comparing new nerve messages with stored memories − are especially important. Messages that flash in an instant through the brain's complex network of association neurons create 'us' − with our attitudes, intelligence, feelings, reactions, mannerisms and judgements.

The most important association area is the prefrontal cortex, found at the front of each frontal lobe (part). This is the 'thinking' part of the brain, involved with learning abilities, intelligence and personality. It enables us to think, imagine, be creative, to plan for the future, solve problems, worry about others and behave in a thoughtful and caring way.

Individuals

Human beings are all alike in appearing human. But we all differ slightly in the way we feel, think and react to situations. This is because our brains are so complex, and each one is 'wired' slightly differently from the next. For each of us, our individual personality is unique: no-one has been just like us in the past, and no-one will be in the future.

Frontal lobe

While all parts of the brain contribute to our personality, the frontal lobes of the cerebrum seem to be especially important. And it is one part of each frontal lobe – the prefrontal cortex – that plays an important part in determining our sense of 'being'.

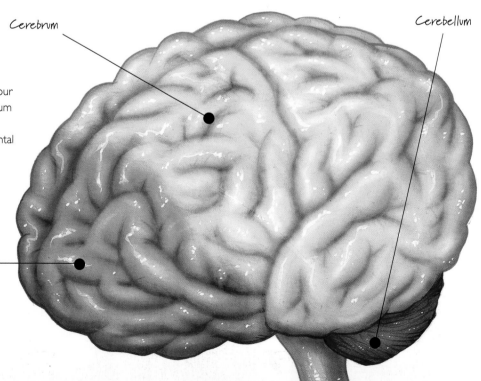

Cerebrum

Cerebellum

Frontal lobe of left cerebral hemisphere

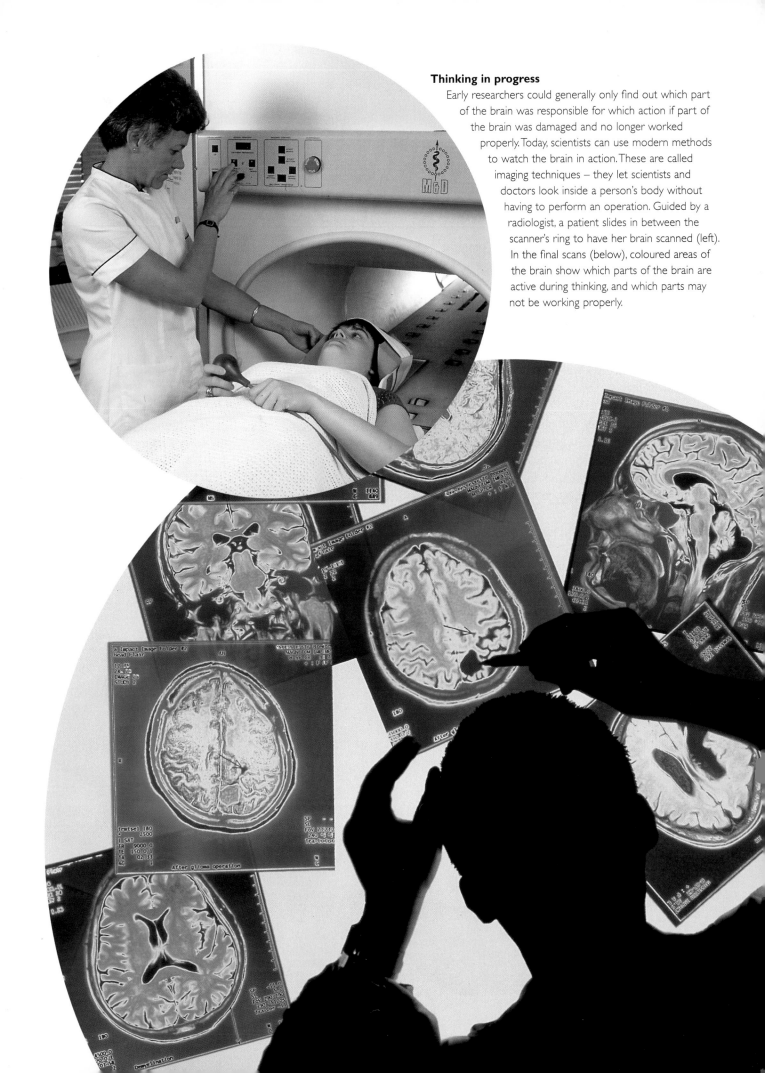

Thinking in progress

Early researchers could generally only find out which part of the brain was responsible for which action if part of the brain was damaged and no longer worked properly. Today, scientists can use modern methods to watch the brain in action. These are called imaging techniques – they let scientists and doctors look inside a person's body without having to perform an operation. Guided by a radiologist, a patient slides in between the scanner's ring to have her brain scanned (left). In the final scans (below), coloured areas of the brain show which parts of the brain are active during thinking, and which parts may not be working properly.

MEMORY

Memory is the ability of the brain to store and recall information. It enables us to remember people and places, to learn from past experiences, and to build up a body of knowledge. Without memory we would be unable to learn.

There are three main types of memory. Sensory memory lasts for just a few seconds. It provides us with a constant awareness of where we are, and enables us to move around without bumping into things.

Short-term or working memory stores nearly everything we experience — but only for a short time. If we look up a telephone number and remember it just long enough to dial the number, we are using short-term memory.

Long-term memory selectively stores information — some trivial, some important — that is remembered for long periods, possibly an entire lifetime. These memories may be fact memories — such as faces, dates or words — or skill memories — such as the ability to ride a bike. Short-term memories may be converted into, and stored as, long-term memories. They may be stored because they are significant, or because they have been rehearsed or repeated.

Where are memories stored?

Memories are not stored in a single location in the brain. They appear to be held in different places. Various regions of the cerebral cortex, for example, are involved in short-term and long-term memory. The prefrontal cortex is responsible for short-lived sensory memory. The hippocampus, part of the limbic system (see page 32), takes some short-term memories from the cortex, turns them into long-term memories, and transfers them back to the cortex where they are stored.

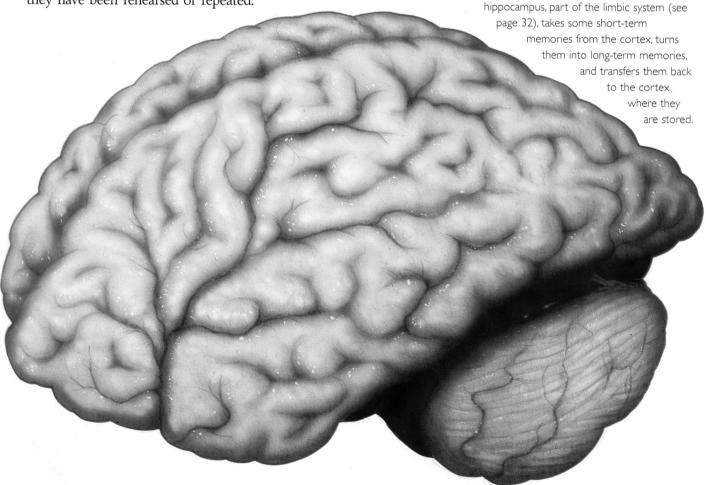

28

Long-term memory

A wonderful holiday, that special birthday party, a good film – all of these are examples of things that stay in the mind, stored in long-term memory. So are facts such as words and dates, and skills like riding a bike or playing a violin. Without them, life would be a blank. Our lives would be meaningless, and civilization impossible.

Sensory memory

Here one second and gone the next, the information stored in sensory memory is very short-lived. It allows us to move around in our surroundings without accident. We notice and remember possible obstacles – usually without thinking about it – and then forget them again.

Short-term memory

Short-term memory can last from a few seconds to several hours. We might use it to look up a telephone number, remember it long enough to to dial it, and then forget it. Much of the information stored in short-term memory is lost, but some of it – if reused, rehearsed, or associated with old memories – may be transferred to long-term memory.

THE BRAIN & LEARNING

Learning is the acquisition of new skills and knowledge. It can happen through instruction or through experience. Learning is a process that continues throughout life, but it is at its fastest during childhood.

The ability to learn is dependent on memory. Physical skills, such as writing or playing football, are learned by trial and error. We try things out, assess how well they work, and store our experiences in the memory. This type of learning may be difficult, but once the skill is acquired it becomes second nature. Facts, figures and language are learned by transferring into the memory information from what has been seen or heard. Such information may be lost if it is not frequently recalled, but the ability to relearn it is always there.

When we are born, we do not have to learn how to learn. The basic learning framework is present in the brain at birth. Learning probably involves the formation of new connections between the billions of association neurons in the brain. When nerve impulses pass along the pathways formed by specific connections, we are able to recall what we have learned. The more stimulation we receive – by teaching or experience – the greater the complexity of connections that form in the brain.

A lifelong process

Learning continues throughout life, but it is in the early years that the brain is at its most adaptable. Through childhood all young humans learn the same basic skills such as walking or running and the ability to speak. Learning is helped by holding, touching and feeling objects. As they get older, children can learn more sophisticated skills such as writing, reading and riding a bicycle. Some children may also learn how to play a musical instrument.

THE PRIMITIVE BRAIN

Have you ever gasped when you touched something cold, clammy and unpleasant? Or felt sad? Or smelled a smell that made you remember something from the past? These experiences and feelings − and those like them − are produced by a part of the brain called the limbic system.

The limbic system is sometimes called the primitive brain. This is because it controls the unconscious and instinctive behaviour that gives us our emotions and helps us to survive. These are very basic, primitive aspects of human behaviour. The limbic system allows us to experience sadness, happiness, anger, calmness, pain, pleasure, fear and rage. It receives information from our senses of sight, hearing, taste, touch and, especially, smell. It has close connections with the cerebrum, the thinking part of the brain, and with memory. These links enable us to associate sensations and thoughts with feelings. The limbic system adds emotional depth to our existence.

Emotion centre

The limbic system is in action whenever we feel pleasure, disappointment, anger, frustration, hope or any of the other emotions that form part of everyday life.

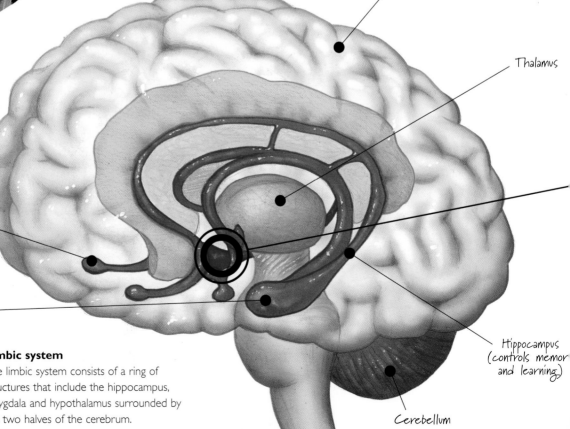

Cerebrum

Thalamus

Olfactory bulb
(controls sense of
smell and links
smell to memory)

Amygdala
(controls emotions
such as anger)

Hippocampus
(controls memory
and learning)

Limbic system

The limbic system consists of a ring of structures that include the hippocampus, amygdala and hypothalamus surrounded by the two halves of the cerebrum.

Cerebellum

Controlling hunger

The hypothalamus determines whether we feel hungry or full up. It receives information from other parts of the brain and the digestive system, and about how much food is being carried in the blood. If we have not eaten for some time, it makes us feel hungry so that we eat. If we have eaten enough food, the hypothalamus stops us feeling hungry.

Hypothalamus

The hypothalamus is about the size of a lump of sugar, and is the body's great regulator. It has links with the autonomic nervous system (see page 38) through which it regulates blood pressure, heart rate, breathing rate, pupil size and the process of digestion. It also regulates body temperature to stay at around 37°Centigrade (98.6°Fahrenheit). It controls both hunger and thirst, and determines our pattern of sleeping and waking. The hypothalamus also links the brain to the endocrine system (see page 40).

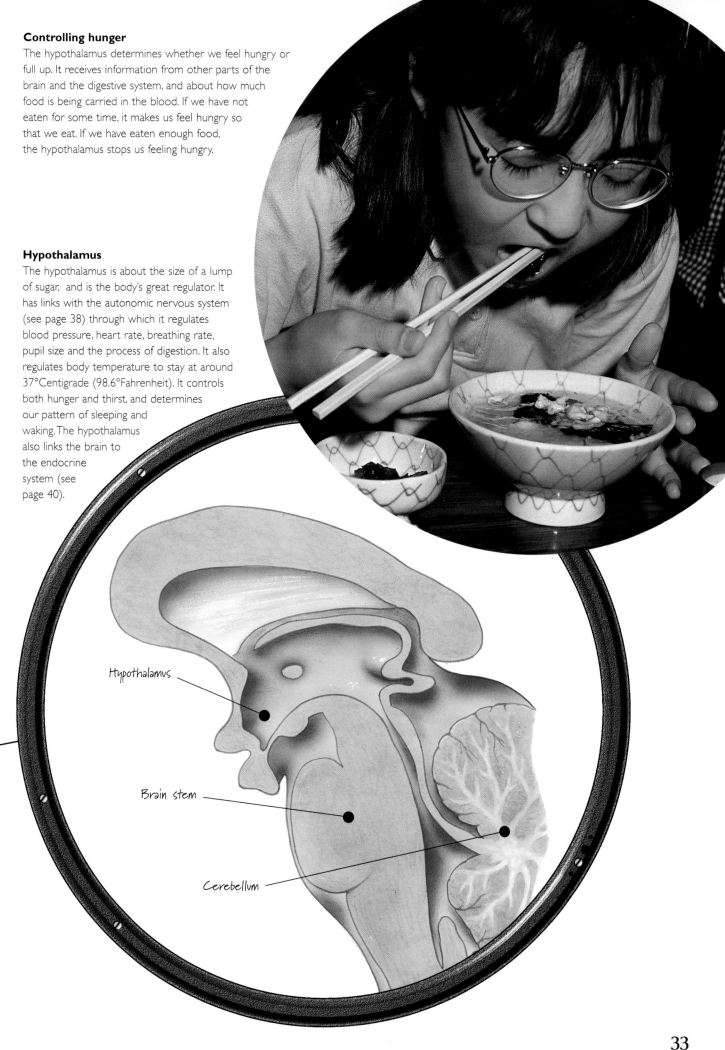

Hypothalamus

Brain stem

Cerebellum

BALANCE & CO-ORDINATION

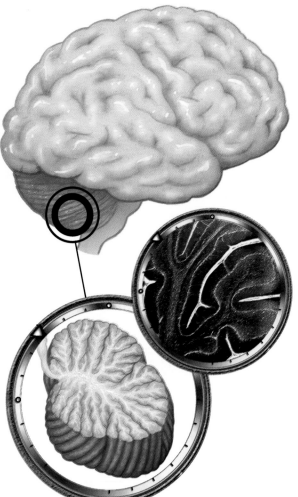

Unlike most other animals, human beings stand on two legs rather than four. This gives us certain advantages – we can use our hands for instance – but it makes us less stable than we would be on four legs.

So, if we are unstable, how do we manage to stand up straight? How do we walk or run without falling over? And how do we manage to perform intricate and complex movements in a smooth and co-ordinated way? The answer lies in our ability to balance and to fine tune all of our movements. The brain receives information from the body's senses that enable it to balance. This information passes to the cerebellum. Here it is processed and passed on to the motor areas of the cerebrum. These send nerve messages to the muscles, which make slight adjustments to the position of different parts of the body. This happens constantly to ensure that we are always balanced. Movement control depends on nerve impulses being relayed to and fro between the motor areas of the cerebrum and the cerebellum.

Smooth movement

When we want to move, the motor areas of the cerebrum send messages to the cerebellum. Here they are modified in response to nerve messages sent from sensors around the body. The cerebellum then relays the fine-tuned nerve messages to the muscles. When the muscles contract, they do so in a way that produces smooth, co-ordinated movements. Without the cerebellum our movements would be jerky and uncontrolled.

Perfect balance

Gymnastics and other skilled movements test the body's balance and co-ordination system to its limits. In order to produce these carefully crafted movements, and to perform such delicate acts of balance, this girl's brain has to process a flurry of information coming from different parts of her body, and then send out instructions by way of her cerebellum so that she can make the next sequence of moves without losing her balance.

Balance pathways

Touch sensors in the skin of the feet indicate whether we are standing up straight or not. Receptors in muscles reveal whether they are causing movement or supporting the body. Information from the eyes shows our position whether we are lying down or standing up. Balance sensors in the ears provide a constant update on our position and direction of movement.

Outer ear

Semicircular canal

Nerve going to brain

Ear canal

Inner ear

Cochlea (hearing part of the ear)

Semicircular canal

Movement sensors

Utricle and saccule

Balance sensors

Inside the ear are two types of balance sensors. Those in the semicircular canals detect movements made by the head when it turns in any direction. Those in the utricle and saccule detect our position in space – whether we are upright or upside down – and something called linear acceleration. You feel this if you are in a car that accelerates very quickly. Nerve impulses from these sensors travel to the brain along the vestibular nerve.

Vestibular nerve

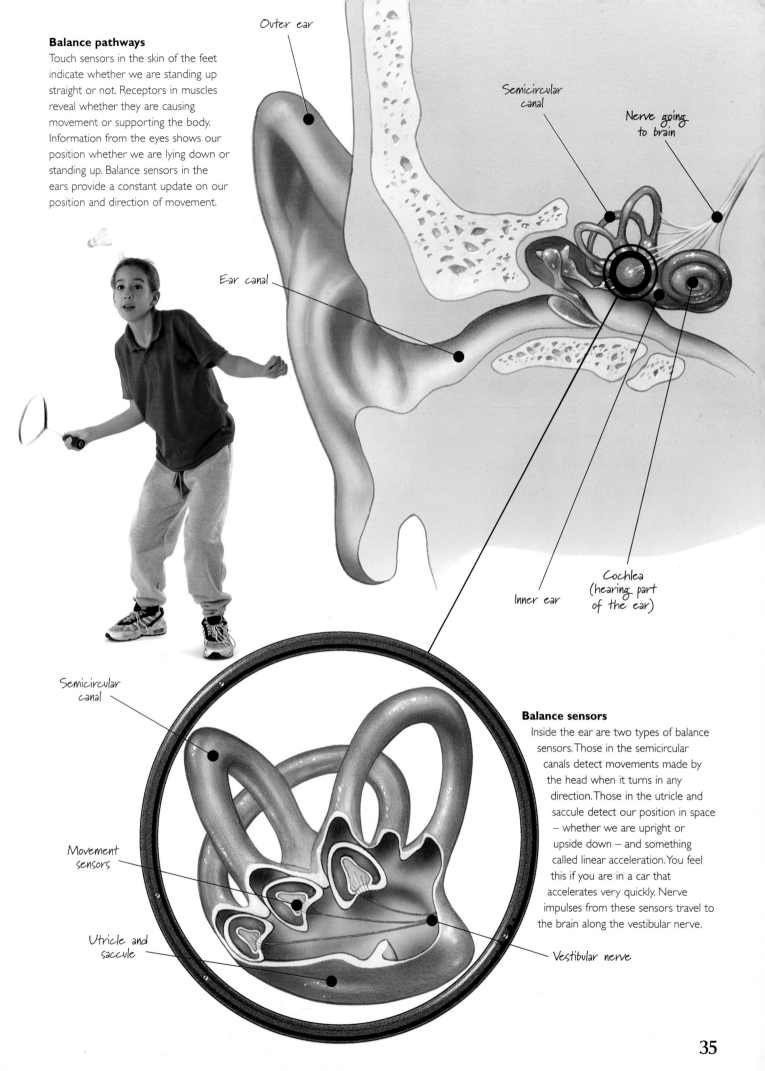

SLEEP & DREAMS

Sleep is something that we all do every day. It takes up about a third of our lives. When we sleep we are neither conscious nor unconscious. We are unaware of our surroundings, but can be awoken by sudden noise or bright light.

The purpose of sleep is to give the body time to rest and repair itself. It also enables the brain to process the day's events, and helps it to learn and remember. Without sleep people rapidly become confused and ill. While we sleep the brain is still active, although its activity is different from waking activity. This is known from studying electrical images of brain waves (called electroencephalograms or EEGs). As we move through alternating periods of light and deep sleep, EEGs show different levels of activity in the brain. Brain waves are most active during light sleep, and the eyes move rapidly under the eyelids. It is during light sleep, also called rapid eye-movement or REM sleep, that we dream. In our dreams we imagine a jumble of events from past and present. This may be due to random activity in the brain, or because the brain is busy processing memories.

What controls sleep?

Sleep is controlled by different parts of the brain. The hypothalamus regulates the timing of sleep: part of it sends us to sleep, and part of it controls how long we sleep. The brain stem also plays a part in determining whether we are asleep or awake, and in dreaming sleep. Finally, the pineal gland produces a hormone called melatonin. This helps to control the daily rhythm of waking and sleeping.

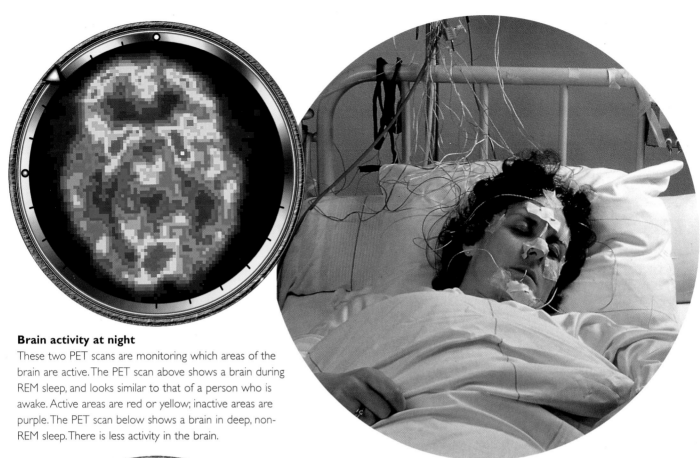

Brain activity at night

These two PET scans are monitoring which areas of the brain are active. The PET scan above shows a brain during REM sleep, and looks similar to that of a person who is awake. Active areas are red or yellow; inactive areas are purple. The PET scan below shows a brain in deep, non-REM sleep. There is less activity in the brain.

Brain waves during sleep

Brain waves are patterns of electrical activity produced by the brain. They are detected using a machine called an electro-encephalogram. This produces a picture or trace of brain waves called an electro-encephalograph (EEG). During the different stages of sleep the brain waves change.

Stages of sleep

This graph shows the pattern of cycles followed while we are asleep. For the first 30–45 minutes of sleep we pass through four stages of non-REM sleep. As we go through each stage, sleep becomes deeper and deeper. After about 90 minutes of sleep, it becomes less deep and REM sleep begins. REM sleep happens about every 90 minutes through the night. After REM sleep, when dreaming occurs, the sleeper goes back to deep sleep. As the night progresses, each period of REM sleep gets longer: the first one lasts about 10 minutes, while the last one is about 50 minutes long.

AUTOMATIC ACTIVITIES

Body activities that take place automatically, without us being aware of them, are controlled by the autonomic nervous system. These activities include releasing saliva into the mouth when we eat food; the pupils of the eye getting wider in dim light; hairs standing on end when we are cold; the heart beating faster when we run for a bus; and muscles in the intestine contracting to push food along it.

Sensors all around the body constantly monitor what is going on inside it. The sensors send this information to the brain and spinal cord. These send nerve impulses along the motor neurons of the autonomic nervous system to organs, glands, blood vessels and the heart. The impulses instruct these parts of the body to regulate their performance and adapt the body to cope with different conditions. For example, if we run for a bus, the autonomic nervous system instructs the heart to beat faster so that more blood is pumped to the muscles.

The autonomic nervous system at work

The autonomic nervous system has two parts: the sympathetic and parasympathetic nervous systems. An example of how they work is the way they control the amount of light entering the eye by adjusting the size of the pupil. (The pupil is the hole that is surrounded by the coloured iris.) Light intensity is detected by sensors in the eye. This information is relayed to the brain. In dim light, sympathetic nerve fibres carry nerve impulses from the brain that stimulate muscle fibres in the iris to contract. This makes the pupils larger so that more light is let in to the eye. In bright light, parasympathetic nerve fibres carry nerve impulses from the brain that stimulate different muscles in the iris to contract. This makes the pupil smaller so that less light is allowed into the eye.

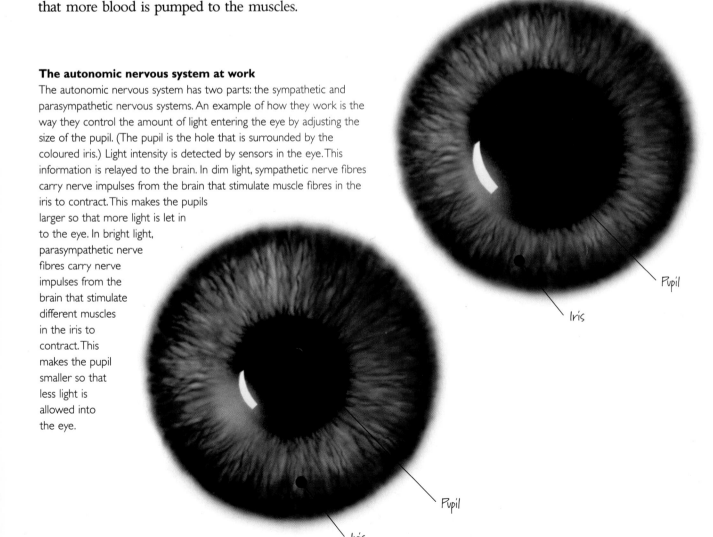

Pupil

Iris

Pupil

Iris

Adjusting to exercise

This athlete is using his muscles to leap over hurdles. To enable him to do this, his muscles need extra food and oxygen to give them more energy. When the athlete starts to run, his sympathetic nervous system automatically increases his heart rate so that more blood carrying food and oxygen is transported to his muscles. After exercise, the parasympathetic nervous system slows the heartbeat back to normal.

Keeping warm

When you are cold goosebumps appear on the skin, and hairs stick out. This effect is created as the sympathetic nervous system stimulates tiny muscles in the skin to pull on hairs.

Eating and digesting

The autonomic nervous system manages most of the activities of the digestive system. It causes muscles to push food along the digestive tract, and makes various glands release secretions such as saliva in the mouth that aid the breakdown of food into tiny particles.

Keeping cool

In hot weather, or during exercise, sweat glands are stimulated by the sympathetic nervous system to release sweat onto the surface of the skin, as seen in this micrograph (above). As sweat evaporates, it draws heat from the skin which cools you down.

39

THE ENDOCRINE SYSTEM

As well as the nervous system, the body has another mechanism to co-ordinate how it functions. This is the endocrine (or hormonal) system. While the nervous system works quickly, the endocrine system works more slowly, and it has longer-lasting effects.

The endocrine system controls a wide range of body activities. These include the amount of urine we produce each day; the body's internal clock that makes us feel sleepy or wide awake; and the way we react to emergencies.

The endocrine system consists of several endocrine glands scattered around the body. A gland is a group of cells that produce and secrete (release) useful substances. Some glands release their products through ducts (tubes) into or onto the body. These include salivary glands, which release saliva into the mouth, and sweat glands, which release sweat onto the skin.

Endocrine glands, on the other hand, have no ducts. They release their products directly into the bloodstream. The substances secreted by endocrine glands are chemicals called hormones. Each gland releases one or more hormones. Hormones are carried around the body by the blood to specific tissues where they have their effect. For this reason hormones are sometimes described as chemical messengers.

Pituitary gland

The pea-sized pituitary gland is located at the base of the brain. It is the most important endocrine gland and releases a number of hormones. Some control body activities directly; these include growth and contraction of the uterus during birth. Other pituitary hormones control the activities of other endocrine glands such as the thyroid gland, the adrenal glands, the testes and the ovaries. The pituitary gland itself is controlled by part of the brain called the hypothalamus. The hypothalamus provides a link between the nervous and endocrine systems. The front part of the pituitary gland makes and releases hormones under instruction from the hypothalamus. The back part stores and releases hormones made in the hypothalamus.

Endocrine glands

There are nine main endocrine glands. Some, such as the adrenal glands, are paired. Males and females have the same endocrine glands apart from their reproductive glands: women have two ovaries; men have two testes. Some endocrine glands also have other functions. The pancreas also produces enzymes that are used in digestion, while the ovaries and testes also produce sex cells (eggs or sperm).

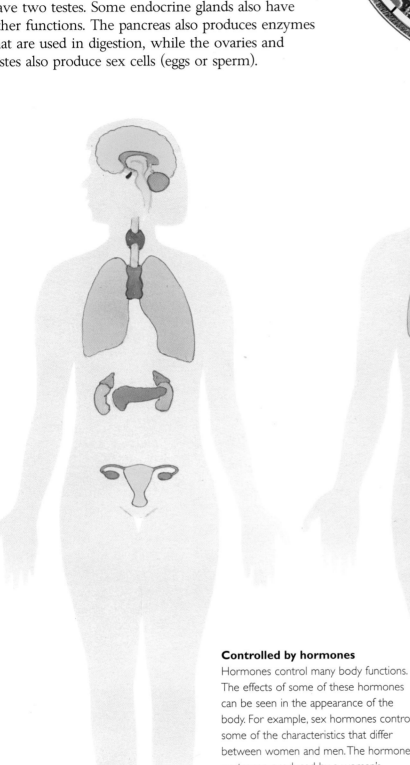

Pituitary cell

This micrograph shows the inside of a cell found in the front part of the pituitary gland. You can see 'packets' of hormones (pink) waiting to be released from the pituitary gland into the bloodstream.

Controlled by hormones

Hormones control many body functions. The effects of some of these hormones can be seen in the appearance of the body. For example, sex hormones control some of the characteristics that differ between women and men. The hormone oestrogen produced by a woman's ovaries give her a rounded shape, while testosterone produced by a man's testes give a more muscular shape with hair on the body and face.

How Hormones Work

Hormones are chemicals produced by the endocrine system. They control certain body processes. There are many different hormones, each with a specific function or functions. After it is released from an endocrine gland, a hormone travels in the blood to all parts of the body. But only certain tissues in the body are sensitive to each particular hormone. These are called target tissues because the hormone is aimed at them.

Target tissues are made up of target cells. Some hormones have broad targets. For example, thyroxine, released by the thyroid gland, speeds up the metabolic rate — the rate at which cells use energy — of all body cells. Other hormones have a single target. For example, prolactin, released by the pituitary gland, stimulates the mammary glands in a woman's breasts to produce milk after she has given birth.

How does a hormone affect a target cell? The target cell has receptor sites into which the hormone fits, just like a key fitting into a lock. Having locked in, the hormone causes chemical changes inside the target cell. This results in a change in the cell's activities, and those of the target tissue.

Hormone action

A hormone is carried by the blood from the endocrine gland that produces it to target tissues that are affected by it.

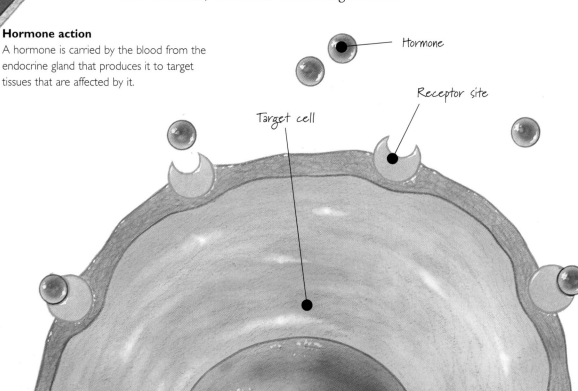

Hormone

Receptor site

Target cell

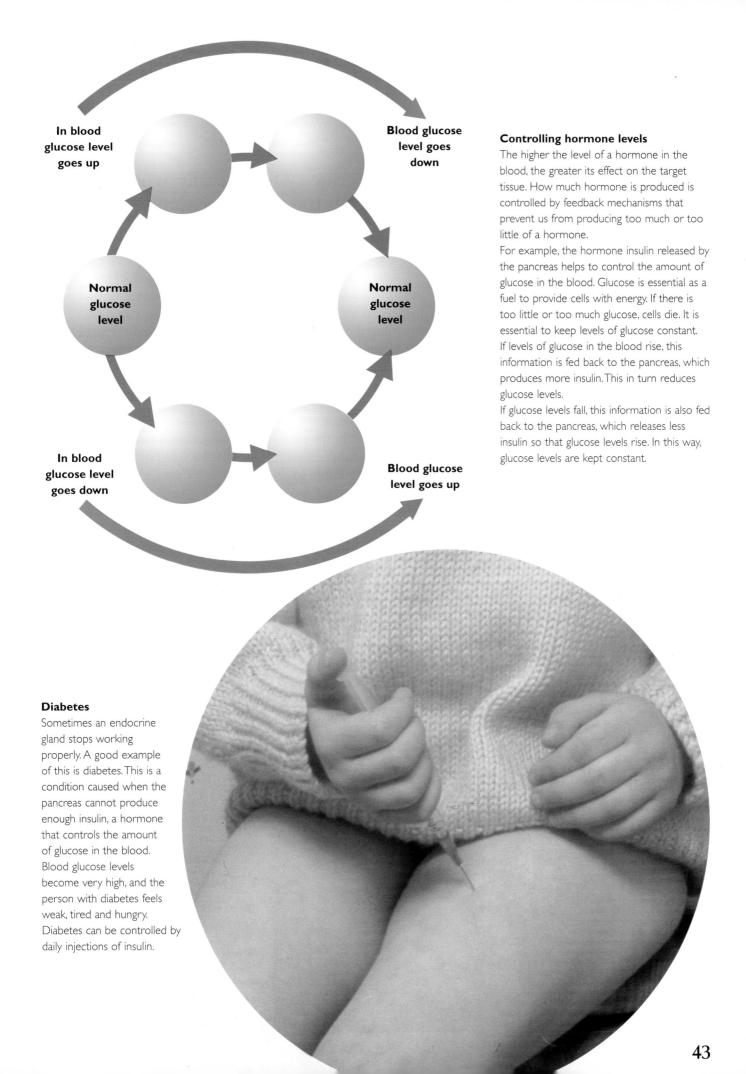

In blood
glucose level
goes up

Blood glucose
level goes
down

Normal
glucose
level

Normal
glucose
level

In blood
glucose level
goes down

Blood glucose
level goes up

Controlling hormone levels

The higher the level of a hormone in the blood, the greater its effect on the target tissue. How much hormone is produced is controlled by feedback mechanisms that prevent us from producing too much or too little of a hormone.

For example, the hormone insulin released by the pancreas helps to control the amount of glucose in the blood. Glucose is essential as a fuel to provide cells with energy. If there is too little or too much glucose, cells die. It is essential to keep levels of glucose constant. If levels of glucose in the blood rise, this information is fed back to the pancreas, which produces more insulin. This in turn reduces glucose levels.

If glucose levels fall, this information is also fed back to the pancreas, which releases less insulin so that glucose levels rise. In this way, glucose levels are kept constant.

Diabetes

Sometimes an endocrine gland stops working properly. A good example of this is diabetes. This is a condition caused when the pancreas cannot produce enough insulin, a hormone that controls the amount of glucose in the blood. Blood glucose levels become very high, and the person with diabetes feels weak, tired and hungry. Diabetes can be controlled by daily injections of insulin.

43

FIGHT OR FLIGHT

Final sprint
As these cyclists catch sight of the winning line in the distance, their adrenal glands release adrenaline to give them extra energy and muscle power for the final sprint.

Dealing with emergencies
Adrenaline works with the nervous system to enable the body to deal with situations which may be frightening or dangerous.

The endocrine system usually works more slowly than the nervous system, and has longer-lasting effects. But there is an exception to this rule.

Adrenaline is a fast-acting hormone that helps the body respond rapidly to emergencies. If you have ever been frightened and have felt your heart pounding, you have experienced one effect of adrenaline. Adrenaline prepares the body to confront a danger (fight) or to run away from it (flight). Its effect is known as the 'fight or flight' reaction.

When the brain senses danger, it sends nerve impulses to the adrenal glands. The adrenal glands are above the kidneys. The adrenal glands immediately release the hormone adrenaline into the bloodstream. Adrenaline travels to several target areas and has certain major effects. These result in more 'fuel', in the form of glucose, and oxygen being made available to muscles so that they can work more powerfully and efficiently. Once the danger has passed, adrenaline is rapidly removed from the bloodstream.

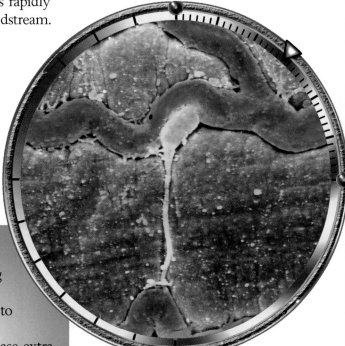

Effects of adrenaline
Adrenaline targets those parts of the body that increase oxygen intake into the body, blood flow to the muscles, and the amount of glucose in the blood.

The major effects of adrenaline:
◆ speeds up breathing and heart rates
◆ diverts extra blood to the muscles
◆ makes the liver release extra glucose (fuel) into the blood
◆ slows down digestion
◆ increases blood pressure
◆ diverts blood away from skin so that the person looks pale

Blood supply
A blood vessel (green) snakes through the skeletal muscle cells. In exercise, blood vessels in muscles widen to increase the blood supply.

Stress
Pressure at work (right) can cause stress. The body reacts to what it sees as danger. But in cases of stress, instead of reacting for a few minutes, the 'fight or flight' reaction carries on all the time. This can make the person ill.

GLOSSARY

Adrenal glands
Hormone-producing (endocrine) glands located on top of the kidneys. They produce a number of hormones including adrenaline, which prepares the body for danger or stress.

Association neuron
Type of neuron that passes nerve impulses from one neuron to another. Most are found in the brain and spinal cord.

Autonomic nervous system
Part of the nervous system that automatically regulates body processes including heart rate.

Axon
Or nerve fibre, the long, very narrow part of a neuron that carries a nerve impulse.

Brain
Control centre of the nervous system. A mass of billions of nerve cells in the head that receives information from all parts of the body, processes it, stores it, and sends out instructions.

Brain stem
Part of the base of the brain that joins the spinal cord and controls basic life functions such as heart rate, breathing rate and blood pressure.

Central nervous system (CNS)
The part of the nervous system that consists of brain and spinal cord. The rest of the nervous system consists of the nerves that carry nerve impulses between the rest of the body and the CNS.

Cerebellum
Part of the brain that lies at the back of the brain behind the brain stem and below the cerebrum. The cerebellum controls balance and helps to co-ordinate movement.

Cerebral cortex
The thin surface layer of the cerebrum which consists of grey matter. The cerebral cortex is where the cerebrum processes information.

Cerebral hemispheres
The two halves of the cerebrum, left and right. The cerebral hemispheres are linked by the corpus callosum.

Cerebrum
The largest part of the brain. The cerebrum is involved in conscious thoughts and actions, emotions and memories.

Electroencephalogram (EEG)
A recording of electrical signals produced by the brain. EEGs can be used to show changes that occur to the brain during sleep, and to check that the brain is working normally.

Endocrine gland
A type of gland that releases substances called hormones directly into the bloodstream. A gland is part of the body that produces a substance or substances that are useful to the body.

Grey matter
Areas of the central nervous system that consist of the cell bodies of neurons.

Hormone
Substance produced by an endocrine gland that acts as a chemical messenger. Hormones are carried by the blood to target cells whose activity they alter.

Hypothalamus
Part of the brain that monitors body activities such as hunger, thirst and body temperature. It sends out instructions via the autonomic nervous system and the pituitary gland.

Limbic system
Part of the brain that controls emotions, such as anger and pleasure, and other aspects of human behaviour.

Motor neuron
Type of neuron that carries nerve impulses from the brain and spinal cord to skeletal muscles and glands.

Nerve
Bundle of nerve fibres that ferries nerve impulses between the central nervous system and all parts of the body.

Nerve impulse
An electrical signal that travels along a neuron. Information is carried through the nervous system in nerve impulses.

Neuron
One of the billions of nerve cells that make up the nervous system. Neurons can carry nerve impulses a long way through the body.

Pancreas
Endocrine gland that releases hormones which control the levels of glucose in the blood. The pancreas also produces enzymes that are involved in digestion.

Pituitary gland
Major endocrine gland, situated beneath the brain, that releases a number of hormones that affect other endocrine glands, or control certain body activities directly.

Reflex
Rapid response that takes place without a person thinking about it. Reflexes protect the body against danger.

Sensory neuron
Type of neuron that carries nerve impulses to the brain and spinal cord from sensors in the skin, eyes, ears, tongue, nose and other parts of the body.

Skeletal muscles
Muscles that are attached to the bones of the skeleton and that move the body.

Spinal cord
Mass of nervous tissue connected to the base of the brain and which runs down the back within the backbone. It relays messages between the brain and the spinal nerves.

Synapse
Junction between two neurons or between a neuron and a muscle fibre (cell). Within the synapse there is a tiny gap between the ends of the neurons.

White matter
Areas of the central nervous system that consist of nerve fibres.

INDEX

Acknowledgements

The publishers wish to thank the following
for supplying photographs:
St Bartholomew's Hospital/Science Photo
Library (SPL) 27 (TL); Biophoto
Associates/SPL 14 (BL); Scott Camazine/SPL
21 (CL, BR), 40 (C); CNRI/SPL back cover
(BL), 3 (BL), 11 (T), 19 (BL, BR); Custom
Medical Stock Photo/SPL 23 (BL); Martin
Dohrn/SPL 39 (CL); Eye of Science/SPL front
cover (BL), 6 (CL), 9 (BR); Dr Don
Fawcett/SPL 12 (TL), 13 (TL); GJLP(CNRI/SPL
6 (TL), 18 (BL); Manfred Kage/SPL 3 (TR), 11
(B), 4 (BL), 34 (TL), 7, 15 (CR); Eamonn
McNulty/SPL 17 (T); Astrid and Hanns-
Frieder Michler/SPL 21 (TR); Miles Kelly
Archives 4 (TR), 18 (TL, CL), 28-9 (T), 34 (B),
39 (TR), 44 (TL); Hank Morgan/SPL front
cover (TR), 31 (BR), 37 (TL, CL); Prof. P
Motta/Dept of Anatomy/University 'La
Sapienza', Rome/SPL 25 (TR), 44 (R); Panos
Pictures 25 (BR), 29 (TC), 32 (TL), 33 (TR),
45 (TL); Alfred Pasieka/SPL 22 (TL);Philippe
Plailly/SPL 18 (BR); Chris Priest and Mark
Clarke/SPL 43 (B); J C Revy/SPL 37
(TR);Science Pictures Ltd/SPL 16 (TL); SPL 6
(B), 9 (BL); Secchi-Lecaque/Roussel-UCLAF-
CNRI/SPL 13 (TR), 41 (TR); Pat Spillane 12-
13 (B, model Puspita McKenzie), 13 (BR), 16-
17 (B), 35 (CL, model Chloe Boulton), 36
(TL, model Chloe Boulton), 44 (BL, models
Puspita McKenzie and Chloe Boulton); James
Stevenson/SPL 30 (BL);The Stock Market 24
(C, BL), 25 (CR), 26 (TL), 29 (TR, CL, BR), 30
(TL), 31 (T, CL, BL,), 32 (CL), 39 (B), 45;
Geoff Tompkinson/SPL front cover (BR), 9
(TR), 20 (TL), 22 (CR), 27 (B); Richard
Wehr/SPL 39 (CR).